Generational Curses

Copyright © 2016 Shannon D. Brown

All rights reserved. No part of this book may be reproduced or transmitted in any form or by any means, electronically or mechanically, including photocopying, recording, or by an information storage and retrieval system without permission in writing from the author of this book.

ISBN-13:
978-1533535658

ISBN-10:
1533535655

Published by:
Minister Shannon D. Brown

Edited by:
Dr. Ruth L. Baskerville

Cover Design by:
B. Jacobs
Miss Shayla D. Brown, Photographer

TABLE OF CONTENTS

Dedication — v

Introduction — vi

Chapter One: A Family's Realization
    God Holds All the Pieces to The Puzzle — 1

Chapter Two: Unity in the Family — 5

Chapter Three: The Prayer Call — 8

Chapter Four: Sarah's Story
    "What Becomes of the Broken-Hearted?" — 13

Chapter Five: Shirley's Story
    From Broken to Healed — 16

Chapter Six: Shyria's Story
    Unforgiveness — 27

Chapter Seven: Shayla's Story
    From Anger to Walking in God's Purpose — 30

Chapter Eight: Shannon's Story
    A Conscious Awareness — 34

Chapter Nine: Mike Jr.'s Story
    From Boyhood to Manhood — 41

Chapter Ten: Patrick's Story
        From Confusion to Clarity   46

Chapter Eleven: Eddie Lee Williams, III's Story
        From Youth to Adulthood Overnight 51

Chapter Twelve: Isaiah's Story
        On the Way to Understanding   56

Epilogue   61

References   64

How to Reach the Author   65

DEDICATION

    I recall as a child the wise words of my father, Eddie Lee Williams, Jr., and I will cherish the twenty-three years God allowed me to have with him. You see, my father developed a heart disease as a child. I believe it was Rheumatic Fever, which is an inflammatory disease that can involve the heart. This disease typically develops two to four weeks after a throat infection.

    He had several open-heart surgeries because of the disease. When he was just eleven years old, he refused the third surgery, and the doctors told him and my grandmother he would never live past the age of twenty-one or bare kids. Nevertheless, he grew to adulthood and had three children.

    So according to the doctors, Eddie Lee Williams, III, Isaiah Williams and me, Shannon Williams Brown, should not be here! God performed three miracles, and four additional blessings, when Daddy also raised Shirley Lollis, Doris McCain, Terrance McCain and Patrick Robinson.

    I dedicate this book to the memory of my father. He was the natural head of our household, and every immediate and extended family member cherished him.

-- Shannon Brown

INTRODUCTION

Repeatedly, God laid upon my heart the charge to unite my family by having all of us go deep inside our hearts and tell our stories of the joy and pain that comes from what I will refer to as a "generational curse."

Generational curses are negative behaviors that are exhibited by family members, and repeated by their children and grandchildren. It is only when we recognize that these curses are spirits warring against us, that we are able to break the cycle of destruction.

For me, I needed God's push to help me write this book. All the members of my family have contributed their very personal testimonies. I believe it has brought unity, as well as an "Agape Love" to all of us. That is the kind of love Christ shows to every man. It's love that is pure and unconditional.

-- Shannon Brown

CHAPTER One
A Family's Realization –
God Holds All the Pieces to the Puzzle

Ever since I can remember, our parents allowed relatives and people they knew to stay in our home. My dad's heart was so big that he wanted to help everybody. Some fell on hard times or became temporarily homeless. In my young mind, everyone was part of a big family, and everyone had a good time.

My mom was only fifteen years old when she gave birth to me. She had married my father when she was fourteen and he was twenty-three. Mom never learned to show affection with hugs and kisses, but I knew she loved me by the things she did for me. On the other hand, Dad always encouraged me and gave me the hugs to go with that encouragement.

The parents never went to church, but always sent us kids with a neighbor. We grew up in church, but everything we saw outside of the church was anything but Godly. It was hypocritical, but at least I can say I learned about God and *The Bible* by attending years of church.

I was a happy child, innocent and playful. I enjoyed chips and ice pops. My young parents indulged me with a steady supply of goodies, and my world was complete.

When I was about five years old, a terrible thing happened to me, but I didn't understand how it would impact me for the rest of my life. My uncle began touching my private parts through my clothes. Of course, I didn't know the word "molestation," but that's what was happening to me.

He used to call me to sit with him and watch a popular Disney musical. I knew all the words, and I loved to sing aloud. He would tickle me and pretend to sing with me. But I felt his hands in places that made me uncomfortable. He used to whisper that our time together was our secret. So I never told anyone about those times.

It didn't take long for me to go from a jovial child to a moody young girl. I talked and laughed less often. Instead, I pretended to be normal so that my parents and siblings would not notice anything wrong with me.

While I believe I was successful at hiding my sad feelings inside, my outward behavior was definitely different. In school, I hesitated to read aloud. I was very defensive when anyone asked me questions. I did have friends, but was always so quiet around the noise they generated that no one noticed my pain.

I remained talkative at home. However, I had the sense to keep my conversations general because, instinctively, I knew I had something to hide. Something had changed in the family dynamic. Distrust entered my world. I became cynical, and I vocalized that I never wanted my parents to invite strangers into our home again.

Mom may have felt that something was wrong with me, but she never would have concluded that I was molested by my uncle. She and Dad did allow fewer folks to stay with us, once I protested pretty loudly. I was too young to understand that I had begun to build walls around my emotions. I may even have appeared angry to everyone in the household.

In front of people, my uncle acted affectionately towards me and everyone else. But when we found ourselves alone, I always ran to my room to avoid being with him. I hated him, and yet I felt helpless to take the step of telling my parents. I don't know why.

Even in middle school, I didn't know how to receive the innocent affection of a boy. This young man asked me out, and I was overcome with a sense of fear and doubt. I made up an excuse not to go with him, and he never asked me anything else again.

I met a group of girlfriends who were chatty and immature. We had fun times attending games and dances. I think they were my little "safe haven" because we saw each other every day at school, and talked on the phone every evening after school. We even walked the streets of Tangelo Park Community together. It was great to laugh and play and be carefree. Sometimes, I almost forgot about the small voice inside of me that carried fear and shame.

By the time I got to high school, specifically tenth grade, I had a girlfriend who liked a boy named Mike. She asked me to talk to him for her. To my surprise, he said, *"Actually, I like you."* He was a senior! He had a kind demeanor and said all the right words to comfort my inner person, even though he had no idea that I had this deep secret.

We were the "alpha couple" in high school, and it was automatically understood by everyone that we would one day marry. I tried to fight falling in love, not wanting to trust any male. Mike was persistent and charming. Before I knew it, I was in love. Mike was, too.

Our relationship grew pretty fast. My dark secret never left me, but it went to a small corner of my mind for years afterwards. Mike had gone off to the service and was gone for the two years that I was a high school junior and senior. He had come home as often as he could to see me, and my heart skipped a beat when I knew he was coming.

On one of his visits, he proposed marriage. As I hugged him hard and cried all over his shirt, he revealed that he had already secured permission and blessings from my dad to wed me. Mike was my first and only true love.

I married my high school sweetheart, Mike Brown, when I was just eighteen years old. It was not a church wedding, but my parents remarked that I looked good after the wedding. They felt that I had chosen wisely!

CHAPTER Two
Unity in the Family

> My first prayer - *The Serenity Prayer*
> *God grant me the serenity*
> *To accept the things I cannot change*
> *The courage to change the things I can*
> *And the wisdom to know the difference.*

After twenty-six years of marriage and two children, I felt God calling to me, saying that my family had "missing pieces" that some would call a "generational curse." It became my charge to break that curse, bind up the enemy, as they say, and bring more family members to Christ in the process.

I remember saying the famous *"Prayer of Serenity"* over and over, as I reflected on that single day in my youth when I realized God had a calling on my life. I was speechless at first, and even a little scared. I had been afraid to join a church because, in my mind, you had to live a perfect, Godly life in order to be accepted into a church. I always felt unworthy because family members drank and smoked and held wild parties.

I was an adult when I learned about spirits and demons that are truly real. They live in the bodies of undisciplined people like my uncle, and they have the power to "jump" to others who are naïve to the world of spirits.

Biblical teachings and guidance from the Holy Spirit revealed to me that I needed to cleanse my body and mind from the spirit of fear and shame. The forum for that was church, which I finally joined at my grandparents' invitation. It wasn't long before I became an active member seeking God for my own deliverance and healing. I soon realized that my feeling of unworthiness was the spirit of fear and of shame that had gripped me and held me captive for decades.

As I started seeing myself becoming "free," I realized that the rest of my family could experience the same freedom if they gave their lives to Christ. I had to find a way to ensure that my whole family went to Heaven with me.

One night I was sobbing, and I knelt down to talk to the Lord. "God, what shall I do to bring my family into alignment with your Word? None of them know you like I do, and I don't know where to begin to explain you to them."

In the middle of my sincere cry to the Lord, He spoke to me! Since giving my whole being to Christ, I many times heard that still, quiet voice that comes directly from God. However, this time, I could actually feel a tenderness and a calm in His words: *"You must be in right standing with Me before you can ask for grace for your family."*

I asked myself, "How do I get in right standing with the Lord?" I didn't get an answer right then, but the following Sunday, while I was in church, an elderly woman sang a song entitled, *"I Want My Heart Right."* I knew instantly that God was speaking to me through this old woman. He was giving me one of the valuable, intangible keys to Heaven.

I began reading God's Word more, praying more, and making special time to be alone with God.

He showed me some of my attributes that were not of Him, like anger, envy and an unforgiving spirit. I acknowledged them all, and asked God to cleanse my heart of them. I changed my thoughts, which changed my actions toward those against whom I had previously exhibited anger, envy and an unforgiving spirit.

Almost immediately, God let me know that I was ready to bring my family to Him in prayer. My phone rang the evening after I asked God to cleanse me, and it was my older sister, Shirley. We were used to speaking daily, but this conversation involved God. Shirley asked if I would be willing to host evening prayers by phone with my grandmother, Katherine, my mother, Sarah, my cousin, Doris, my sister, Shirley and her daughter, Shyria, and my daughter, Shayla.

Shirley had never before asked me to pray with her, much less to pray with four generations of the broken women in our family. I knew God was behind it all, but I was still nervous and excited about the prospect of all these women of different ages coming together for a common purpose. I quickly said, "Yes. I will pray with all of you, beginning tonight." God literally changed all of our hearts simultaneously, and we've been chasing after him from that moment.

CHAPTER Three
The Prayer Call

At 9:00 p.m. nightly, the six women from four generations of my family agreed to conduct a phone conversation that we called the "Prayer Call." The format was simple. We began our first Prayer Call with me asking if any of us had any prayer requests. My grandmother, Katherine, said that she didn't have a prayer request at that time, but she wanted to thank God for answering one of her prayers.

"The women in our family are finally establishing true relationships with Christ, and that is the beginning of breaking the generational curses that are upon us. I'm so grateful that we've all agreed to pray together every night." I was stunned by my grandmother's words because she had never opened up about her truths, and here it was our very first "Prayer Call."

It was supposed to be an opening prayer, maybe a scripture reading, and candid dialogue among the women on the call. However, it turned into my grandmother, Katherine's confession about her whole life. The rest of us listened intently without a word of interruption.

"Y'all know I'm the matriarch of this family. And you know that I was just seventeen when I delivered my daughter, Sarah, followed by Uncle Otis when I was eighteen. What some of you didn't know was that Uncle Otis molested both my granddaughters. Actually, he raped Shirley, but he also touched

Shannon." I heard a few gasps on the phone, but no one said a word. Personally, I was glad this was coming out because our family kept secrets about the molestation that had been going on in our family for generations. Katherine continued.

"I admit I was a bit of a 'wild child,' and chose to leave my kids with an aunt while I went from Alabama to Orlando, chasing a no good man. I thought I was in love, and I realize now that there is no excuse for leaving my children."

Katherine went on to tell us that her first husband was named Uncle Otis Reeves, Sr., and they married in Orlando. She separated from him and went back for her kids. Sarah was her oldest child, and at that time, Sarah was five years old.

Back then, families had what is called a 'sister cousin,' and Doris was that person. She was Katherine's sister's daughter. Katherine met her second husband, Herbert, and went to Carolina. *"One weekend, my son, Willie, found a .22 caliber shotgun and loaded it for my protection from Herbert.*

Herbert could be described as mean, from birth to death. He beat his children and often hit and verbally abused me, too. He came home one particular night, cursing and threatening me. He was coming towards me to harm me, when I remembered the loaded gun. I reached for it and shot Herbert. He died instantly. I'm not proud of this, ya'll, but God has put on my heart to tell you everything."

Katherine told us that she spent ninety days in jail, but was not charged with murder. She believed God forgave her for this murder, and He also kept her from being prosecuted for the murder of an evil man, father and husband.

Herbert' son was named Harry McCleary, and everyone knew that Harry was the biological father of my sister, Shirley. My grandmother, Katherine spoke directly to Shirley at this point in our Prayer Call. *"Harry had the mean spirit of his Dad, and kidnapped you, Shirley in order to get you away from the only family you ever knew. I don't know if you remember, but he took you to his mother's home. Your Mom, Sarah, had to get the police involved in order to get you back. After that, Harry disappeared."*

Katherine kept talking. She said she married again, this time to Walter Lee Morgan. She met him while both were in jail. Both were considered model prisoners and given the title "Trustee in Prison." Katherine got out first, and waited for Walter to be released. They married, and the first few years were good. Walter was good to my Mom, Sarah, and my Uncle, Willie.

Walter soon cheated on Katherine, and when she found out, she separated from her third husband. What he brought to the family that Katherine said was "a positive" was that he made sure my siblings and I went to church regularly. As a matter of fact, we were in church nightly.

Katherine and Walter went to Georgia, and my childhood memories included visiting them in the summers. Soon after, the family realized that Walter was a hypocrite, pushing church and religion on his family, while openly behaving in a heathen manner. Still, it gave the grandchildren a foundation of what church was like. We "played church" when we were not actually in church, often mocking Walter through role-playing. *"My grandchildren thought they could play church behind my back, but I knew what was going on. Truth is I agree that he was a hypocrite."*

Katherine continued to share with the women on the call that she left Walter and found her next husband, Eugene Thompson. They stayed together a decade, during which time my Mom, Sarah, and Uncle Willie became adults. Eugene came into the marriage with children, and Katherine said that he took their side against her when there were disagreements. *"My grand kids, along with Eugene's children, always remembered much fussing and arguing during that period. Wish I could have stopped it, but that was the life."*

Katherine admitted to us that she was known for choosing men in her life who were flawed, and she thought she needed to marry all of them. Her last husband was Paul Williams, whom she called "the best." He gave her much attention during their seventeen-year marriage and their thirty-year relationship. He died March 27, 2014.

My grandmother, Katherine ended the story of her life by making a profound statement to the effect that it was only after Paul died that she focused exclusively on God and her family. She confessed that the spiritual strength we were now hearing for the first time on this Prayer Call was due to God revealing Himself to her when she lost Paul.

There was a long pause where none of us spoke, but we could tell that each of us was reflecting on how awesome God is when He moves in His own timing. I took the lead to bring closure to our conversation, since I initiated the Prayer Call idea. "Grandma Katherine, I know I speak for everyone on this call when I say that you have given us all strength to deal directly with our demons, and to be candid with one another about what we really felt at different times in our lives when bad things happened to us. Let's pray."

I surprised myself with the length and depth of my prayer, but no one interrupted or made the kind of noise that would let me know I better get to "Amen." At last, I said, "Amen," and we expressed love for each other before hanging up. I believe we were all excited for the next Prayer Call, where we could say what we've been holding inside for way too long. Expressing feelings of love out loud was something most of us had kept buried for years. We were changing!

CHAPTER Four
Sarah's Story
"What Becomes of the Broken-Hearted?"

The following night at 9:00 pm, we came together once again on our Prayer Call, and I prayed that we would have a productive session that continued to bring healing to the family. Before I could speak another word, my mother, Sarah Williams, Grandma Katherine's daughter, said she must speak the truth, but with love towards her mother. She said she had not slept well last night, thinking about all that her Mom shared.

Sarah began: *"Mama, I always loved you, but I have some anger inside me that's been building up since I was a child. I feel ready now to let it go, because of your openness and honesty last night in the Prayer Call. I didn't understand why neither you nor my father was there to protect me from being raped when I was twelve. I think I even hated you both for a while, but I never said anything.*

I was only thirteen years old when my Shirley was born. I only had two periods when mean ole' Herbert's nasty son, Harry raped me, right in our house. He hurt me and I cried, but he never stopped. I don't remember if he threatened to hurt me more if I told, but I didn't tell you, Mama, because there was already too much confusion in the house."

Sarah didn't want to tell Katherine how sad and confused she was by Harry's act because she thought it would only cause more family problems. *"There was already constant fussing and fighting because of the drinking and not enough of money. Besides, both of us lived in the house, so that meant no one was leaving. I was thirteen and pregnant. Barely understood what the word meant because you never talked to me about sex, Mama."*

Sarah told everyone that she decided that instead of telling Katherine about the rape, she would leave Alabama to go and live with her Auntie Virginia in Florida. No one suspected Sarah was hiding a secret as big as having a baby, so Katherine let her go.

Auntie Virginia allowed Sarah to keep her pregnancy from her Mom until she was about to deliver her daughter, Shirley. That's when they both told Katherine. I knew my grandmother was going to interrupt Sarah right here. *"I'm sorry you were raped, Sarah, but you never gave me a chance to take your part with that no good Harry. I'm still hurt that you assumed I wouldn't care, or I wouldn't do anything. But mostly, I'm hurt that you never told me you were pregnant before you left for Florida.*

I wonder if you can imagine how surprised and angry and upset I was when your Auntie Virginia called me and said my daughter, Sarah needed to talk to me. You were about to deliver my grandbaby, and I was hearing about it for the first time. I thought I got over it, but right now, I'm angry all over again. Got to pray for God to take that feeling out of me."

Sarah delivered Shirley three months early, probably because Sarah had no real prenatal care. Folks like us in the South, most using midwives to deliver our babies, didn't know much about the right prenatal care, and those of us who did couldn't afford it. Sarah reminded all of us on the call that Shirley was only three pounds at birth.

I interjected, "My older sister, Shirley was a fighter from birth." *"That's what I'm talking about, Shug,"* Shirley replied. Everyone laughed a little. But then Sarah turned the conversation serious again. Everyone knew she only got to the eighth grade, but we didn't really understand why she didn't go back and finish school.

She explained, *"All y'all know that Auntie Virginia wasn't a strong woman now, and if I didn't bring up the subject of finishing middle school and going all the way through high school, Auntie wasn't thinking about it. Anyway, she said if I was grown enough to have a child, I was all the way grown! No more schooling was necessary. I didn't know it at the time, but it was the biggest mistake of my life."*

CHAPTER Five
Shirley's Story
From Broken to Healed

Shirley was one of four children, and her siblings were Eddie, Jr., Isaiah and Shannon, called "Shug." She was molested by the same uncle who later inappropriately touched baby sister, Shannon.

We later learned that Uncle Otis had also been molested as a child, and this could explain why he handled his pain by inflicting pain on others. When I think of the power of generational curses, I feel very sad to realize that it impacted some of the men, as well as the women in my family.

I recall a passage in the *Holy Bible,* where a holy person casts the spirit of a generational curse out, sending it to a dark, dry place. *"Then he (spirit) saith, I will return into my house from whence I came out; and when he is come, he findeth it empty, swept, and garnished. Then goes he, taketh with himself seven other spirits more wicked than himself, and they enter in and dwell there; and the last state of that man is worse than the first. Even so shall it be also unto this wicked generation."* Matthew 12: 44-45.

To me, this means that, if one of my relatives were strong enough, and aware enough of the power of Satan, he or she might have cast that spirit out. However, without the help of the Holy Ghost, none of us would have been strong enough to keep that evil spirit from gaining strength and returning to harm the next generation of my family.

Uncle Otis was a perfect example of this some years ago, but he is beginning to seek the Lord God for his own healing. He has already recognized the harm he caused Shirley and me, which I will detail later in this book.

Uncle Otis traumatized Shirley from age five until thirteen, but she never told anyone because she thought it was normal. In fifth grade, she realized it was wrong when she sat in a health class watching a video on sex education.

The video described a "normal" relationship between a man and a woman, where sex had a positive connotation. There was no shame or fear, so Shirley was puzzled at first. Then, as if God literally dropped the truth into her spirit, Shirley screamed silently. There was nothing normal about what her Uncle Uncle Otis was doing to her. It was wrong and sordid, and she felt ashamed and dirty. What had *she* done?

Still, she couldn't confide in her parents or her siblings. Instead, she harbored that shame and guilt for something she thought SHE had done wrong, and withdrew from everyone at home and at school. I remember when we were small, Shirley used to wet the bed, and Mom chastised her physically and verbally, trying to make her stop.

Shirley probably didn't even know why she was wetting her bed, but she continued the habit until she was about sixteen and I was fourteen. In retrospect, I realize she was crying for help during all the years of being abused by Uncle Otis. None of us had any reason to think something deeply painful was happening to Shirley.

Shirley had started working with our Mom at the age of thirteen, cleaning guest rooms and folding linen in the laundry room of a hotel. She thought she was grown and didn't need to focus on school. After all, she was making her own money while her peers were getting allowances from their parents.

Shirley said, *"Hey, at that time, I was purchasing my own drugs, and I bought all my own clothes. Really, I did what I wanted to do. I couldn't related to what was going on in school, even though my Mom was adamant about her kids finishing high school. She never even finished the middle school, you know.*

But then I got pregnant at sixteen, so I stopped going to school. I never stopped using drugs, of course, and that resulted in my having a "stillborn" child. I regret losing that baby to this day." That sent her deeper into drugs, as an escape from a young life filled with more pain than a teen should have to endure.

Her then boyfriend went to Kansas, where his family lived. Thinking her only option was to join him, Shirley went to Kansas, but found another dysfunctional family. So she left for Arizona, where the boy's father lived.

It was July 26, 1986 when Shirley's boyfriend joined the military. That was also the date of my birth. Shirley had married her boyfriend before he left, but now she returned home to Florida. Soon he sent for her, since he was stationed in Alaska. They were there for four years, during which time she had a daughter and lost our father within three of those years. Regrettably, Shirley had not seen her father in five years, when she invited him to visit, and he said, "Yes."

Shirley described her father as *"a good husband and father. We talked every Sunday, and he was getting ready to visit me in Virginia when my husband and I transferred to Alaska. Dad never made it to either place."*

Shirley's husband, Sherman, was never faithful. *"I remember always needing to be high in order to have sex. I never experienced a healthy marriage – didn't even know what one was supposed to look like. The things I know today, if I had known them earlier, I would have been married longer. I had so much fear and hate, confusion and shame inside of me that when I married, I had no idea how to love a man."*

Shirley went on to share how each time she tried to become intimate with her husband, she saw her uncle. *"Each time Sherman wanted to be intimate, I always had to be high. If it wasn't drinking, it was weed or smoking marijuana or crack, or snorting powder. Sometimes, I used all of them together. I got high daily for years, and the addiction escalated until I gave up all the drugs except crack-cocaine, which I used non-stop for ten years before I got sober."*

Shirley explained one particularly painful day in her life as an addict. *"There was a big family argument because I became friends with some crack buddies. I left my daughter, Shyria with my Mom, who put her to bed. Shyria woke looking for me, and I was gone. My Mom couldn't console her, so she cried herself back to sleep.*

The next day, I came home and they said I left her all day and night and she was crying and looking for me. The police had been called, and the moment I walked through the front door, two officers wanted to talk to me. I was still high, and now I was also hungry and very tired. I didn't want to talk to anyone, much less the cops.

I walked away, but one of the officers tried to stop me by grabbing my arm. Shyria became enraged and tried to bite and kick him. The other officer intervened by lifting Shyria off the floor and strongly placing her on the floor next to my Mom. Since I'm her mother, I was charged with battery on a law enforcement officer, all because I didn't want to listen."

Shirley shook her head and lowered her eyes, as if regretting the whole incident. She was, in fact, arrested and jailed for at least three months. However, God was at work! In prison, they offered a class in Bible Study, and Shirley took the class. She remembered how we were all raised in church, and now she realized that she needed God's help to turn her life around. *"Train up a child in the way he should go, and when he is old, he will not depart from it."* KJV Proverbs 22:6.

While in jail, Shirley became keenly aware of her spiritual roots. She was very knowledgeable about the *Holy Bible*, and she excelled. She then started going to church services, too. The whole experience reconnected her to her roots in Jesus Christ. She vowed to give up drugs, once she got out of prison.

When she got out, she tried really hard to give up crack cocaine, but she was unsuccessful. Shirley went right back to heavily using drugs. The *Holy Bible* quickly became a distant memory once more.

Predictably, Shirley went to jail again for probation violation, this time asking to go into a drug recovery program which would shorten her jail time. She was accepted into the program. One of the trustees from the prison church encouraged her to stay on the path towards being drug-free.

Although Shirley finished the recovery program, and had her sentence shortened, she couldn't stay away from drugs once she got out. So, she fell prey to her addiction again. Shirley recalled that right after she returned to using drugs, her Mom insisting that she sit at the kitchen table and pay close attention. *"I'm telling you something for your own good. If these drugs are killing people we know in the streets, what makes you think it won't do you like the rest of the people you see?"* Stubborn Shirley quickly replied, *"No way. Ain't gonna do me that way 'cause I can handle it."*

Of course, Mom was right and Shirley was wrong. Once Shirley saw that she couldn't overcome her weakness for drugs, even though she did manage to stay out of jail, she went to Virginia, where her husband, Sherman was. They spent three years there, while he finished his military tour, and he received an Honorable Discharge.

However, Sherman continued to cheat on Shirley during this time, so they split up for good because of it. Shirley had few options, so she left Virginia and moved to Pennsylvania to work with Mom again. She put forth much effort during working hours, but the moment her work day ended, Shirley and her "sister cousin," Doris, borrowed cars and went to buy drugs. Both of them were serious users of crack-cocaine. I suspect our Mom knew the truth, but didn't want to face this harsh fact about her child.

Once there was no more work in Pennsylvania, Mom and Shirley moved back to Orlando. Sadly, that brought them back to the old neighborhood in Tangelo Park, where illegal drugs and alcohol were prevalent. A person with a stronger constitution than Shirley would have had a difficult time resisting drugs, so this bad environment, coupled with the fact that Shirley knew all the drug pushers, made it impossible for her to stay off drugs.

Shirley must have stolen goods from friends' homes, but for the first time, she began stealing items from Mom's home to sell for drugs. When Mom couldn't take it any longer, she told Shirley she would have to leave. Shirley became homeless, bouncing from one friend to another, or living temporarily in abandoned houses.

Living on the streets of Tangelo Park, she met a guy named Johnny, who allowed her to move into his house. Now she had a bed and clean sheets. However, she still trolled the streets daily in search of drugs, and an African-American female officer stopped her six times within two hours. To Shirley, this was harassment, and she boldly let the officer know her feelings. I'm convinced that this, too, was the presence of God in my sister's life. He had a plan for her, and wasn't going to let her destroy her life completely.

Finally, the officer promised to arrest Shirley if she had to stop her one more time to check for drugs. On that sixth time, the officer kept her word and arrested Shirley for possession of paraphernalia. Sure enough, Shirley found herself back in the same jail she had been in twice before. She met the same people as before, and noted to herself that it was like she never left. It was right before Christmas.

"Lord, I can't keep doin' this. This be the last time I'll find myself in this place. When I get out, I'm gonna get high just one more time, and then I promise myself I'm getting into a drug rehab program. Promise, God!"

Shirley stayed in jail a short time for this minor offense, and, true to her word, as soon as she got out, she found the drugs to get high "one more time." God literally granted her wish, but He did it His way. *"God allowed me to get high one more time, just like I wanted. But He didn't tell me I was gonna hallucinate! I was out of my mind and acting crazy! I thought I was gonna die that night."*

What was really happening, I believe, was that God used that African-American female officer to cause Shirley to go to jail for what would be her last time ever. She needed to go there so she could repent once more, and promise God that if He let her get high just once more, she would turn her life around and quit drugs permanently. As Shirley described herself, *"I was running from the person who turned out to be ME. Imagine that!"*

Shirley actually had an epiphany at that pivotal moment in her life. In the midst of a terrible, haunting hallucination, Shirley cried out loud to God: *"God, people tell me that you're real. If you are, show me something right now. Right now! I heard a voice talking to me, and I saw a hand shining bright as noonday sun. 'Shirley, if you grab hold of my hand, I promise to lead you and guide you in the spiritual realm.' I said, 'Show me what to do and I'll do it.'*

Then, the hallucinations stopped, just like that. I was sweating and crying and disoriented, like I was in a trance. But I remembered everything God said – everything!"

Shirley came straight to my front door, knocking frantically. She couldn't contain her nervous excitement, but blurted out incoherent sentences about being touched by God. She said, *"Shyria's birthday is just two days from today, and I just got out of jail – again! I'm going to recovery."*

Honestly, Shirley had made similar promises so many times before, and we had talked so much about her need to get clean and sober, especially for her daughter, Shyria. She never managed to keep her promises. Sarcastically, I asked, "How are you going to pay for it?"

Shirley looked back at me, determined to get help this time. She said she didn't know how she could pay for rehabilitation, but nothing was going to stop her this time. I began to believe her now. She asked me if she could use my phone to call her daughter for her birthday, and I gave her the phone. I couldn't help overhear the whole conversation because she never walked away. Maybe she wanted me to hear her words.

"Shy, I'm so sorry that I've been nothing but a bad mother for the last seven or eight years. I have nothing to give you for your birthday, but all I can offer you is a clean and sober Mom. If you give me one more chance to be a real Mom, I won't fail you." Shyria responded without a moment's hesitation, *"I'll take it and you know you can't take this back."* Even though Shirley had made this promise too many times to me, this was the first time I heard her plea

for her daughter's forgiveness and patience as she overcame her addiction.

Rather than to let Shirley leave my sight, Mike and I had her stay with us while we secured the help she needed. The last thing Shirley said to me before we left her for a while was that she remembered taking a hard look at the men who hung out at her usual crack house, and who had always appeared as friends in drugs together. This last time, she saw them as disfigured monsters. That would be God!

Shirley also heard directly from God for the first time, when she uttered that she had no idea where to start to change her life. He spoke to her in a soft voice, saying, *"I'm going to use you to bring people out of what I am delivering you from."*

Mike and I had gone to our local church, where we had been members and tithers for years. Our Pastor agreed to help us secure space at a facility in St. Pete, Florida, and he added that since we had been such faithful tithers, the church would incur the expenses for Shirley's care. Within two days, Mike and I were driving Shirley to the recovery center.

During the two-hour ride, Shirley shared a number of confessions about her life. She shared the second time God spoke to her, in response to her question about how she got on drugs in the first place. *"Shirley, you don't know how to deal with hurts, trauma and pain, all connected to the sexual abuse you experienced as a young child. You buried your feelings deep inside, but now I will help you bring them forth so you can heal."*

When we arrived at the facility, a very kind and efficient staff greeted us. They showed Shirley to her room, and spoke to all of us together about what her life would be like for the next six months. A rehabilitation facility chaplain took Shirley's hands and asked to pray with her. She said she didn't remember how to pray or seek God's forgiveness for years of bad living, and for terribly neglecting her child.

The Chaplain told her to lift her hands and tell the Lord that she surrenders her life to Him. I can say that it's been nine years since that trip to St. Pete, and Shirley has maintained an intimate relationship with God and never gone back to using crack-cocaine.

Shirley captured the feelings of most family members by saying that all of the adult female family members were convinced there had been a generational curse on the men and women in the whole family. Part of the reason for sharing their pain through the chapters in this book was to pronounce the end to the curse of family dysfunction and sexual abuse.

Shirley – my beautiful sister who is dark-skinned, and short with big hips, always smiling and "shownuff sassy." The Lord truly restored my sister's life and health after a 21-year bout with crack-cocaine. Today she is a woman of God who is loving, passionate and caring for others. She is a "straight to the point" person who loves to see lives changed by our Lord and Savior.

CHAPTER Six
Shyria's Story
Unforgiveness

Shirley's daughter, Shyria moved around the country because her father, Sherman, was in the military. Sherman and Shirley initially moved from Orlando to Alaska, then to Tennessee, and finally to Virginia. When Shirley decided to leave Sherman, due to his infidelity, the couple decided that Shyria would have a more stable life living with her Dad. Shyria thought back to the first remembrance of her Mom's drug use. *"I really didn't notice things until age six, when we had our water or electricity cut off. I didn't know why, but I knew it had to do with my Mom.*

During the time I lived in Virginia, my Dad had a lady friend. I stayed with them until I was ten, but almost as soon as I got there, I was molested by my Dad's girlfriend's son. They had tried to make one room as two, with little divider hanging to give the impression that we had separate bedrooms. It didn't work, apparently."

This was the first time Shyria opened up about anything that happened while she stayed with her Dad and his lady friend. No one knew until she revealed it, that Shyria, too, had been molested. *"At first, I was picked on a bit. The son bullied me and beat me up when my Dad wasn't around. I told Dad, but no one did much of anything. Dad was too wrapped in his lady friend, and that hurt my heart."*

Shyria admitted that she was molested more than once, and didn't tell anybody for years. She painfully revealed how she was having problems using public rest rooms, and how she was almost grown, but found herself sometimes wetting the bed.

I knew something was wrong, but desperately hoped that Shyria had not been molested. However, the Holy Spirit spoke to me, revealing the sad truth that she had, in fact, been hurt by the man she now told everyone about. It may have started even before this, with any of the men who regularly frequented her Mom, Shirley's home during the time they all used drugs.

Shyria said without emotion that the experience with her Dad's girlfriend's son made her hate men forever. *"I tried to have a boyfriend once, but it didn't work. Mom turned her life around and told me to try talking to a therapist. I told her I would be all right, I'm my own therapist."*

Shyria went through high school, but didn't get her diploma because of half a credit. *"I tried to get my Dad to go to the school on my behalf. There was a racist teacher, and I was switched from my math class in that last year. The new teacher wasn't like the one I had, who was helping me, and she failed me. All the Black kids that year didn't pass in her class."* She vows to go back to school eventually to finish it, hopefully soon.

Shrya's mood changed to include a little bitterness, as she continued to talk about her relationship with her father. *"My Dad married his girlfriend, and I didn't like that one bit. It's like I felt for a long time he chose her over me. So I said I would kill myself, or move out just to get their attention, because from age 12 – 18, it was just my Dad and me. When he wanted to get married again, he just* shut me out. I did everything in my power to make them both miserable, but in the end the only one miserable was me."

Still, I went back to live with them for a short time after my bad high school experience. He told me a fairy tale -- that he would help me get my diploma through a program called 500 Reach. He would help me get a place and get back and forth to school. I had no transportation, so when Dad stopped, I couldn't get to school. So that didn't work."

Shyria did a number of minimum-wage jobs, watching others with high school diplomas get promotions while she remained at the same level of employment. She knew she could do most jobs better than her peers, but without credentials, she was limited.

Finally, she got a job she could tolerate. It was at a bar and grill. She became a cook, and the kitchen staff members are showing her different positions related to preparing food. She seems to like this job enough to stay awhile, but recognizes the need to get that high school diploma.

"I'm close to my Mom. Believe it or not, when people go through with parents doing drugs and not being there for their children, they don't have good relationships. I never lost faith in my Mom, so we have a good relationship. I'm the only child. I don't go to church much, but I do pray."

Shyria has a long-term relationship with a woman she believes may one day be parent to her unborn children. She trusts her companion, and believes her companion has her best interest at heart. *"I'm moving on with my life. Maybe one day, I'll forgive my Dad, but not today."*

CHAPTER Seven
Shayla's Story
From Anger to Walking in God's Purpose

"I didn't know about Mom telling Dad to never touch me, from the time I was born. Now I realize why my Dad and I were never close growing up. I didn't think he loved me because he never hugged me." Shayla said she was always watchful of men around her because she had been told about her mom and aunt being molested by their uncle.

She was never close to him, and didn't know that he was the one who molested her mom and aunt. But she always felt an eerie sense being around this uncle. *"I remember Mom telling me to lock myself in the bathroom when she had to leave me with Grandma to babysit. My uncle lived there, so I see now why Mom was cautious. But since she didn't share the truth with me earlier, I was just scared of him."*

Shayla then recalled some unpleasant details about what her Mom called a "generational curse." *"My grandmother in Alabama was also molested. I learned about this after I found out about my mom and my aunt being molested. I've always hated roller coaster rides and the heart-dropping feeling I got riding them. Whenever I was about to hear some really bad news, my heart dropped the same way as when I rode the roller coaster. I got that exact same feeling when I started to piece everything together. The whole thing made me fearful."*

Shayla was sad when the family moved to Apopka as she began middle school. She missed all her elementary school friends, and in the new school, she befriended two girls who were already best friends. One of the friends had a boyfriend who talked to all three of them, but the girlfriend hated Shayla because her boyfriend seemed more interested in Shayla than her.

The two best friends went against Shayla in the end, which made no sense. Shayla experienced bullying, mostly from these girls, but also from other mean students. *"I recall one night, they called my house phone and tried to argue with me. My Mom had to get on the phone and threaten to call the police if they didn't stop harassing her daughter."* So Shayla left that school after one year.

Shayla's second year of middle school was at a location a block from her home. Too many of the 7th graders were wild, engaging in drugs, sex and parties. So Shayla coped with this by becoming quieter than she had been. *"When my older brother, 'Little Mike' graduated from high school and had a girlfriend, I know I slipped into depression. Although we didn't spend much time doing the same things, I always knew he was a presence close by, just in case I needed him. Now, he was wrapped up in this girl, and I felt like I was losing that steady support that I needed around me."*

Shayla continued. *"I opened up to my Mom about feeling depressed. The advice she gave me was, 'You gain the heart of a champion when you learn to be alone.' I didn't understand the meaning right away, but her words lingered in my mind. I felt a little better, like there was hope."* Shayla and her Dad, Mike had begun to repair their broken relationship during this time.

When it came time for high school, Shayla was afraid to go, and she wanted Virtual School. Nevertheless, she decided to give public high school a chance. At first she liked it, but then fell back into depression and loneliness. *"Whenever I was at school, I always felt heavy-hearted. I sensed I was alone, even though I was around hundreds of people. It seemed I was the only one there."* During this time, Shayla hung around with one best friend and a cousin.

In 10th grade, Shayla's great-grandfather died. He and her great-grandmother, Katherine, were living in Shayla's home. Because Katherine was ill and frail, she didn't want to be alone. So she asked her son, Uncle Otis to stay with her during the day. Shayla was angry because each day when she came home from school, her uncle was there. She knew clearly what he had done many years ago, and though he never attempted to touch Shayla, she resented him being in her home. *"I was so angry with him, so I found a reason to be angry with everyone around me. It was a dark time in my life."*

Shayla revealed that this was a time she didn't pray as much as she usually did, but embraced the negative feelings. She actually wrote a tearful letter to a talk show called *"Fix My Life,"* hoping hers would be chosen to start the process of healing her family. She never sent the letter, but just writing her deepest thoughts began her personal reconciliation with her family.

In 11th grade, she joined Student Government Association and planned all the school events for the year. She got to be creative, and felt that the thirty-three people in Student Government were like a family.

Shayla was a serious student, and she decided she wanted to graduate early. So she had a full load of courses in her junior year, plus virtual classes, plus summer school just before the third year of high school began. All of that allowed her to graduate high school at age seventeen. She is now in college, majoring in Business. She is focused on God as the center of her life.

At the same time, Shayla is working on developing a healthy relationship with a male friend. A few young men who've been attracted to her have had personal issues, but they appreciated the fact that she carried herself as a Christian young woman. She was actually able to lead them into a stronger relationship with Christ.

Shayla's Mom, Shannon, described her as her "young, beautiful, freckle-faced daughter, who is light-skinned with a thin build, long red hair and glasses." Shannon is most proud of the moral character that her lovely daughter possesses, as she enters the adult world.

CHAPTER Eight
Shannon's Story
A Conscious Awareness

As Shannon turned to religion for comfort, her sister turned to drugs, and Shannon began to cry as she explained her pain at seeing her sister "on the streets" or even "in the streets," strung out on drugs. There were years where Shannon felt no one could reach her sister's heart, nor change her destructive behavior.

At some point in their young adult relationship, Shannon and her sister revealed what terrible things their uncle had done to each of them. Shannon was first to realize they needed to do something collectively about the whole situation, or both of them would descend into a life of heartbreak and sin. So the sisters determined to share the truth with their mother, who moved from hearing the news with incredulous expressions on her face, to believing her daughters and feeling deep remorse at not herself seeing what must have been evidenced right in front of her eyes. Shannon's sister entered drug rehab, and has remained drug-free for nine years.

"I felt as if I was living in the light, while my sister was living in darkness for all of those years. As I rose higher in education and work opportunities, my sister sank further into despair. It hurt me so badly, but there was nothing I could think to do at that time."

It was through the prayers of Shannon, Mike, family and friends that her sister, Shirley first went to rehab. "God elevated Mike and me, and we were aware that our spiritual walk was getting deeper. Yet everything around our nuclear family was not spiritual, and some of it was even chaotic. I was certain at one point that God was speaking directly to me. He told me that my sister and I needed to address, but not confront our uncle at the same time.

We rehearsed what we would say, changing our words several times before we finally decided on the date and time to ask him to see us. He must have known the contents of the proposed meeting before it began, because he was remorseful enough to cry before we finished telling him how dirty and confused he made us feel. Our uncle was in his 50s by this time in our lives."

Shannon went on to explain how she and her sister forgave their uncle, because God assured them that the only way they could completely recover from years of trauma was to forgive their uncle without reservation. He started coming to church with his nieces, and Shannon believes he gave his life to Christ at some point.

She articulated the difficult time she had verbalizing the words, "I....we forgive you, Uncle." But in the end, her words were genuine, and the forgiveness was real and total. Shannon and her sister, Shirley felt God's presence approving of what they had done.

During the period of time where Shannon struggled with when and how to share the news of the molestation of herself and her sister, and to then actually forgive the relative who had abused them, Shannon led a fairly normal life.

Shannon and Mike had a son, and four years later, a daughter. It was right then that she blurted out to he husband, "Don't you EVER touch our daughter inappropriately, or I think I could actually kill you!" In truth, she had forgiven the abusive uncle, but in her heart, she feared that all men, in general, might take physical advantage of all women, even girls who might be their daughters! Mike was at first stunned, never seeing that side of his wife before. Shannon had always been meek and slow to anger, always keeping a positive disposition. When Shannon showed with her body language that she would stand by her ultimatum to the death, her loving husband had to make the emotional adjustment to understand her feelings, and not his own.

    She was a devoted and loyal wife, so these words cut through Mike like a knife. He asked his wife where this venomous comment came from, and through tears, Shannon reached all the way back into her youngest memories to bring forth all the pain, sorrow, horror and shame associated with what her uncle had done to her over many years. Instantly, Mike understood why she threatened him, and Mike held Shannon tightly and vowed never to inappropriately touch their daughter.

    Shannon confessed something she felt badly about. "I think that moment impressed something unintended on Mike, and I regret that to this day. When Shayla was a baby, Mike held her and played with her, hugging and kissing her as often as he wanted. I watched as she got to pre-teens, and suddenly, Mike stopped touching her affectionately. I knew he was afraid of being accused of doing something wrong, and I didn't know how to tell him I had confidence in him as a Dad who would never touch his daughter in a bad way. But I couldn't find the words, so I said nothing, and watched my daughter and husband grow farther and farther apart."

Shannon tearfully recounted the time Shayla turned sixteen and got her driver's permit. Mike and Shannon were in the financial position to purchase a car for their daughter, and in the midst of all their joy, Mike cautioned Shayla not to drive in unsafe places, to always watch the road and not be distracted, and on, and on, and on,.... Shayla burst into tears and said, *"Why do you care what I do? You never loved me. You don't even hug me! You have nothing to say to me about driving safely, Daddy."*

Shannon said she had to tell Mike, "HUG YOUR DAUGHTER!" He never hugged his son, Mike, Jr., either, though. The first time he showed public affection was when Mike, Jr. graduated from the Air Force Academy. After the ceremony, his father embraced him, and both men shared a deeply affectionate moment together.

Shannon added, however, that for all the years of their marriage, Mike was always affectionate towards her. Perhaps he felt safe giving unconditional love to his wife, but sensed a need for severely limiting his demonstrations of love for his kids. He always loved them....always.

Mike, who never had a father figure to show him the complexity of being a real man, always provided for his family. He thought that was the essence of his father/husband responsibilities. He never imagined more was required of him as a parent.

Shannon sat the family down one evening, presenting them with God's assessment of their family as having "missing pieces." Each confessed all the unsavory behaviors they had engaged in, and everyone cried as they shared the most honest moments in all four of their lives. Mike, Jr. had experimented with drugs, held a gun, and admitted he might have gone down the sad path of so many of our African-American youth, except for his home training.

Shayla assured her parents that she believed in marriage before sex, that she had aspirations for an early high school graduation and college after that. Mike admitted that he had been drinking more often than his family realized, which gradually led to his being a heavy drinker. Shannon had been the rock of the family for as long as she could remember, and listened intently to her family's candid confessions.

Shayla did, in fact, graduate early from high school, and entered college in good standing. Mike, Jr. felt God had given him a vision to open a business selling tee shirts. It's called *"Young and Wealthy,"* and those words appear on all the individually designed tee shirts. Mike, Jr. had been kicked out of his public high school, and ended up in a Christian school -- the best thing that could have happened to him. There were strong male figures mentoring and guiding Mike, Jr. at the new school.

Although all the family had been in church regularly, they re-dedicated their lives to Christ at that moment, collectively and individually. The result was that a permanent bond was formed among persons who, to that point, had only co-existed together in the form of a family. "We each dedicated our lives to Christ, knowing that we had to work out our salvation with fear and trembling."

Around that time, husband, Mike's drinking had increased to a dangerous point. He was driving home and caused an accident. Though he wasn't hurt, the driver of the other car jumped out and punched Mike in the mouth. Mike fled the scene, coming straight home and telling Shannon what had happened. The next morning, the police arrived to give Mike a summons, but because he had a busted lip to prove the other driver punched him, he was not charged with leaving the scene of an accident. Shannon gave him an ultimatum that he must either choose his drinking or his family.

From that day, Mike never took another drink. He received no counseling or AA support, but God... just God's favor. Shannon realized that her family needed to leave Tangelo Park, Florida, in order to save her family from the unproductive life so many in that area experienced every day. She felt God was leading her family to move to Atlanta, Georgia.

The family did move to Atlanta, and stayed there six months, during which time they expanded their spiritual awareness and befriended a few strong Christians who encouraged their faith walk. Although in Atlanta for only a short time, Shannon and Mile realized that God had directed Shannon's family to move back to the Orlando area, this time in a new community in Apopka. The move back home brought Shannon's family in contact with her uncle again, since he never married or left her Mom's home.

Shannon's maternal grandparents moved into the new home which Mike and Shannon had purchased. Shannon's mother, uncle and cousin purchased a home in the Apopka area close by. Healing between Shannon's uncle and the rest of the family began in earnest, once all of them were living in close proximity to each other. Shannon believes, in retrospect, that once again, God was the orchestrator of causing the grandparents to move into their grandchildren's home. And that brought the uncle back, too.

When both grandparents were alive, Shannon dutifully drove them to their home church before going to her own. However, once her grandfather passed, she persuaded her grandmother, Katherine to come to church with her and her family. God was working yet another miracle for everyone, because Shannon's uncle and cousin came to church and became saved. Maybe everything that was terrible in Shannon's early years was her preparation for the role she now played as the matriarch and spiritual head of these blended households.

She contemplated writing a book about her life, possibly called *HEAL MY FAMILY*. Shannon's daily prayer to God is, "Lord I don't know what you have in store for me. Please just make, shape, and mold my family into the individuals you would have us to be. Heaven is what I want for my family, as well as myself, Lord." Then she shed tears of joy, thinking about the place she is in her life right now, because God is truly answering every one of her prayers.

CHAPTER Nine
Mike, Jr.'s Story
From Boyhood to Manhood

Shannon recalled the day she and Mike had their first child. "Our son, Mike Jr. changed our lives forever when he was born. We were two people in love who God entrusted to be parents over this little life. From the first moment this child looked into his father's eyes, Mike wanted to be a better person, and the best possible father to his newborn son.

Almost from the time Mike, Jr. could walk, he and his dad played basketball. The whole family attended nearly every basketball game, once Mike Jr. became a sports star in elementary school. He remained competitive and talented throughout his middle and high school years.

During Mike, Jr.'s tenth grade summer, he watched Dell Curry's basketball training video. Uncle Pat had brought Mike, Jr. the video because he thought it would enhance his nephew's basketball skills. *"After the video, I had this burning urge to push myself to be the best I could physically be. I quickly grabbed my basketball and jogged swiftly to the neighborhood YMCA with shear determination on my mind."*

Once Mike, Jr. arrived at the gym, he darted straight past the check-in desk and walked through the two-door threshold leading to the court. *"I had one thing on my mind: to practice. No distractions, no excuses, and no quitting. I endured five complete hours of pushing my body past what I thought was my physical peak. I continuously shot the ball, until* my arms felt like they were no longer a part of my body.

I picked up my basketball off the freshly waxed hardwood floor and prepared myself physically and mentally for the biggest game of my life the following week. This particular experience, thanks to my Uncle Pat, taught me practice plays a major role in all life's endeavors."

Mike, Jr. recalled the most important basketball game of his life. "UHRRRRR!!! I can still remember the sound like it was yesterday. The scoreboard buzzer blaring off as loud as a block party in New York City, and for the last thirty-two minutes, I had been in a state of bliss. Drenched in sweat from head to toe, muscles aching, and out of breath I stood at the center of the basketball court, feeling the best I had felt all week.

Despite the screams and chaos going on, I could only hear my Dad's elongated baritone voice screaming, "be aggressiveeee" "shoot the ballllllll" "Go to the holeeeee"! I can still hear my father's voice yelling at the top of his lungs from the bleachers. The bleachers were filled with what seemed like two hundred and fifty people.

I wanted badly to look in the direction of my Dad for encouragement, but I kept my mind and eyes focused on the ball. I held my breath, raised my arms, and tossed the ball in what seemed like a slow motion dancer. The crowd became hushed, as all eyes followed the ball until it landed right through the net without touching the rim. Nothin' but net!

I finished the game with 20 pts. and the entire gym surrounded me at half-court to congratulate me on a game well played. The energy from the crowd's *excitement propelled my feeling of serenity and this is a moment I will always cherish. It was the proudest day of my life."*

Throughout Mike, Jr.'s high school years, the basketball court had served as almost a place of therapy for him. *"Time after time, I have been able to visit the basketball court and prevail through any situation I was facing. The basketball court has taught me three significant life values: practice, aggressiveness, and serenity."*

On more than one occasion, Mike, Jr. was worried sick about the health of his great-grandparents. *"I felt like I was in a place as dark as an abandoned warehouse with no windows. Basketball was the only thing I could do to place my struggles out of my mind for the time being. It was my release during the time when both my great-grandparents were going back and forth to the doctor and the hospital."*

While Mike, Jr. did win the biggest game of the season in his tenth grade year, he also experienced what athletes call *"the agony of defeat."* Mike, Jr. realized after his thrilling success on the basketball court that his fans expected the same level of performance forever. He may have expected the same level of excellence, too.

Mike, Jr. shared a personally painful time in his teens when he couldn't match his stellar accomplishment the previous school year. *"Even though I had a terrific tenth grade year in sports, I was still a little timid and afraid to make mistakes on the court. I remember this one time where my father had driven me down to Tampa on a Friday evening for a weekend basketball tournament.*

I had practiced enough to do well, but something inside of me gave me an uneasy feeling about winning this game. My confidence was gone. Sure enough, I lost the game, and I felt I had let my dad down in that moment."

Mike, Jr. then recounted the sadness he felt when he went on to lose every game since the first in that season. *"This was a devastating 'Mike Tyson-like' blow to myself confidence. My father noticed the frustration and shame on my sweat-filled face, and told me not to get too down on myself.*

On the silent ride back home, all I heard was the A/C blowing on full blast, until my father finally looked over at me and said, 'You have a lot of potential. Where is the confidence that spilled out of you all last year?' I thought for a moment, and finally found the words to say that I was afraid I could never be as successful as I was that one season. It was a special moment in time, and I guess I was scared I couldn't match it."

Mike, Sr. assured his son that he loved him unconditionally, that he should not try to emulate past successes, but only to play aggressively and leave it all out on the court. *"That is all anybody can ask of you, Son."* His dad's words really resonated in his heart during that long, emotional ride back home from a losing game. To this day, Mike, Jr. considers himself to aggressive in every aspect of his young adult life.

"Having such varied experiences growing up on the basketball court, I now visit the court anytime I need a minute to clear my head. When you find such

a place like the one I have, you should cherish and visit that place as much as you can."

Shannon describes her first child and only son this way: Mike, Jr. is a very ambitious young man who aspires to own his own business. He is in the Air Force Reserves, working part time and running a small T-shirt business. He states the Lord gave him the name for his business -- Young and Wealthy, and it represents, not just wealth in money, but also wealth in dreams that inspire persons to be rich in knowledge, culture and diversity.

I have watched him grow from this shy boy into the proud young man he is today. He's my young, average build, light-skinned, freckle-faced, muscle bound son! My Mike, Jr. keeps his black hair trimmed in a nice high top fade with waves, and everyone always says he looks just like me! I agree!!"

CHAPTER Ten
Patrick's Story
From Confusion to Clarity

Patrick was the child raised with Shirley, Ike and Shannon, but who was not biologically connected to any of them. Sarah became his guardian/Godmother when his biological mother and father gave him to Sarah when he was just six months old. Patrick's mother had worked with Sarah, and trusted her to take care of Patrick and raise him to manhood.

Everyone babysat Patrick, including Sarah, Shannon, Shirley and some cousins. He remained in communication with his biological parents during his growing up, and because he didn't understand how to cope with abandonment, even in the face of having a "normal" family around him, he resented his natural parents for fifteen years before forgiving them. His real mother had six children and gave the first four away to different people. She kept the last two.

Patrick's mother had a nervous breakdown, after it appeared that mental problems in the family had skipped two generations. The illness caused her to realize she couldn't raise her children at that time in her life. So, in her mind, she did the best thing for them by giving them to trusted people.

When Patrick was a small child, he was happy being around so many who loved him. He was unaware of the true nature of not having his biological parents in his life. However, when he became a teenager, some family members and friends began to question him about having a different last name from the family name. He really didn't know why he had a different name, because the subject had never come up and his "family" provided a nurturing environment for all the children in the house. They didn't consider Patrick to be different in any way.

Nevertheless, Patrick began to internalize feelings of confusion and abandonment. He wanted answers, but was unable to verbalize the questions. His schoolwork slipped, and he became distant in school and at home. He seemed disinterested in everything except video games. It was his escape from a reality he neither fully comprehended nor wanted to accept.

Shannon recalled, "My Dad took special care of Patrick all his life. He brought him chocolate milk everyday because it was Patrick's favorite drink. He spent quality time with him, fostering the male bonding that comes when father and son get haircuts, go shopping, and talk while riding in the car together."

Patrick did love Shannon's father very much. He admired the fact that his new Dad went to work everyday. He was curious about his Dad's profession of being a shoemaker. Sometimes, Dad came home with some of his work, and taught Patrick and the other kids to stitch soles on shoes. It was fascinating, since none of the kids knew how shoes were made.

While Patrick grew close to his Dad, he adored big sister Shannon. And when her boyfriend, Mike came on the scene, he was very happy to receive double the attention. Shannon even felt a little like Patrick was her child. She took time to tend to his needs, including going to a favorite spot –

McDonalds, and going shopping. You could say Shannon and Mike really spoiled Patrick.

When Shannon married Mike while both were in their late teens, the dynamic among Shannon, Mike and Patrick changed. Patrick became a little sad initially because the couple with whom he had spent much time had now left home to start their own lives. Even though Patrick had not fully dealt with his inner feelings of abandonment by his birth mother, something about "losing" Shannon and Mike brought him sadness.

During Patrick's middle school years, he felt depressed about having "two families." He felt alone in the midst of family gatherings. He wanted to run away and keep going to someplace far away. So he walked the halls of his school, skipped classes and then skipped school altogether. Only math grades were good because math came easily to Patrick.

Patrick is almost thirty years old now, still confused and angry because it's hard to put his life together in any order that makes sense to him. Part of the reason for what might be called a sudden shift in Patrick's attitude as a teen was that when Shannon's Dad died, the obituary listed all the family members with the same last name of "Williams," except for Patrick. He saw the name "Patrick Robinson" for the first time in print, and it disturbed him greatly. It hit him hard to know for certain that he was adopted.

He began to aggressively seek answers about his birth, and while he was ready to hear the truth, the family was uncomfortable telling him the truth because life isn't all "black and white." How do adults explain the "gray" area to children? So, the adults gave vague responses to Patrick's increasing inquiries, which bothered him further.

Shannon remembered one particular day when Patrick, then thirteen years old, came from school demanding to know the truth of his lineage. Shannon's Mom, Sarah told him he had "two moms." She revealed that Patrick's real mother lived locally, and Sarah promised to take him to visit. Thereafter, Sarah took Patrick a couple of times a month to see his biological Mom. Patrick even got to meet his two younger half-siblings, with whom he formed a good relationship.

Patrick was feeling better about his past after being able to begin a relationship with his natural mother and siblings. His paternal grandmother, Bev, who also lived close by, made it a point to stay in touch with Patrick at least twice a year.

It was Bev who took Patrick to Jamaica to see his biological father, and the first time Patrick met his Dad, Ron, it was like seeing himself in a mirror. The resemblance was unmistakable.

Patrick was not a child who normally showed much emotion, especially in public. However, instead of rejecting his father, Patrick literally embraced him, and the two developed a strong bond from that moment.

His father had four kids, including a five-year old daughter. Patrick volunteered that he also had a five-year old daughter! Both men were shocked at each other's news at first, but once the information was shared, they kind of laughed about a father and son having a child – a daughter -- the same age.

While Patrick seemed to have found some peace finally meeting his immediate family, he suffered the long-term effects that come from being born into a dysfunctional home. Patrick remains unmarried, having moved in and out of relationships without being able to commit to one woman. He believes that is because of his early confusion about his true lineage. "I have to admit that I have abandonment issues, and it's hard for me to love or care for anyone wholeheartedly."

Patrick admitted that he spent years blaming others for his behavior, rather than trying to understand the circumstances surrounding his parents giving him to another family. Also, he confessed that he was still learning about himself and developing an appreciation for the childhood he did have. He realized how blessed he was to have grown up in the caring, stable environment with parents like Sarah and Eddie, Jr., and with siblings like Shannon, Shirley, Isaiah, and Terry.

CHAPTER Eleven
Eddie Lee Williams, III
From Youth to Adulthood Overnight

Shannon introduced Eddie Lee Williams, III. "He is my older brother, actually my "half brother, having the same father as I." Eddie Lee was not raised in the household with Shannon and her other siblings. However, every summer and all holidays were spent with all the children together. Eddie Lee was happy when he was with his brothers and sisters, especially since he was his mother's only child.

"I was born 1967 in Monticello, FL, and when I came home to Greenville, FL, I lived with my mother and her parents. As I was growing up, I lost my Mom at the age of eleven years old. I stayed on the family farm, as the only child, and my grandparents finished raising me."

When Eddie Lee was about seven years old, his mom decided to leave the area. He didn't want to go with her, so she left him in the capable hands of her parents. She returned from time to time, but Eddie Lee had gotten attached to his grandparents and didn't miss his mother much. *"So I missed her a little, as my Mom. But grandmother was 'Mama' too."*

Eddie Lee's Mom was living a fast life and running with an unsavory crowd. *"One night we were called to hear she was in a fight and had been stabbed. They told us they didn't know her condition, but she was actually dead at that time. It seems she and another woman were friends who had gone out together, and Mom refused to give a cigarette to the woman. She followed my Mom into the restroom and stabbed her repeatedly."*

Eddie Lee called his Dad because he was so broken up about the senseless murder of his Mom. Shannon and the rest of the family knew of the horrible incident, but none really knew Eddie Lee's mother. He was especially sad because his Mom was only twenty-five years old when she died, and the incident happened on Valentine's Day.

Eddie volunteered, *"My Mom was the type who always dressed well, and liked to have a good time. The lady who killed her was jealous. She asked for a cigarette, and just because Mom said 'No,' she followed her and stabbed her for that. Really it was her jealousy though. My Mom was prettier and more popular, but now she's dead. Every Valentine's Day, I get really sad. But life does go on.*

I still have the article in the newspaper about it, and the woman went to jail. I had hatred in my heart and wanted to kill her. But I realized it was the wrong thing to do. I had to forgive her. I turned to my Bible for solace, and I guess God led me straight to Matthew 6:14-15: 'For if ye forgive men their trespasses, your heavenly Father will also forgive you. But if ye forgive not men their trespasses, neither will your Father forgive your trespasses.' Yeah, I had to forgive this woman."

I guess Eddie Lee could say that "the apple didn't fall far from the tree," because he, too, was a wild child. His grandmother was, no doubt, worried and disappointed with the choices he was making in his earlier years. *"I did have a history of being with women, and I ended up having four kids and grandkids by three women. But I have always taken care of my kids – always. Anyway, the Lord brought me out of all of that. Mind you, I had to seek Him, since He wasn't looking for me right then. Having God in my life is the best thing to happen to me."*

Eddie Lee is not married, but says he has a wonderful fiancé, and they've been together seven years. His grandmother talked about wishing his Mom could have lived to see the type of man he turned out to be. *"I'm still seeing after my grandmother, who is 102 years old, and she understands me so well. I've had some rough times, and done some things I regret. But Granny stayed there with me through everything. Oh, yeah, I love her."*

Eddie Lee said that all the kids are grown, and he has eleven grandkids. They all live in the same town, so he gets to see his offspring all the time. Eddie Lee made it clear that he will always be a presence in the lives of his children and grandchildren.

Eddie Lee spoke about his maternal grandmother, who was Eddie Lee, Jr.'s mother. *"My granny was a woman I could tell all my problems to. I remember times I sat with Granny and talked with her about some pretty deep stuff. When I left her, I felt better because she was a sweetheart. She was very affectionate and I needed that.*

Shannon's Mom, Sarah, treated me just like I was one of them, even though I never called her 'Mom.' I used to look forward to visiting that whole family because there was a stable environment in the house. During the long summers when I visited my Dad and Sarah, he would talk to me about being my father, and he gave me pointers on life. Even though I had a happy life with my grandparents, I wished I could also have grown up with Shannon and her siblings, to be closer to my Dad."

Eddie Lee revealed to his son that there were things he didn't know about or do with his Dad. He told his son he wanted him to know everything about him. As a result of him being so candid and approachable with his boy, the two built a good relationship.

Eddie Lee reminisced about the time he had a football scholarship to college. He was really excited about going to college, but he felt the need to stay with and protect his grandmother. Because of his decision to support someone other than himself, Eddie Lee is convinced that God gave him favor.

"You know what? God is blessing me. I was in church, but not saved. What caused me to get saved was I was coming home from work one day and saw my friend get killed by truck hitting him on a motorcycle. It did something to me. I realized life is fleeting, and I joined the church that next Sunday.

Sometimes, we fall short, but I have been in the Men's Ministry, and I'm faithful in attendance. One of my sons stayed with me until he got grown, and I brought him to church. My grandkids go to church with their parents and with me.

No, I can't say I am generally satisfied with my life because I feel like there is room for improvement for me. I used to tell my sister, Shannon, I don't worry about happiness. I say, it's nonsense because I go back to my decision to stay with my grandmother. A lot of times, there's things I want to do, but I don't do *them because of her. And I don't regret it. I'm the one to take care of the whole family."*

CHAPTER Twelve
Isaiah's Story
On the Way to Understanding

Isaiah is Shannon's brother, two years her senior, but younger than Shirley. The family on her Mom's side had some history of mental health disorder, and she believes that Isaiah may be the last member to exhibit deviant behavior. Shannon's earliest serious interaction with Isaiah was when she was four years old and he was six. He hit her hard across her head with a *Coca Cola* bottle. His intended target may not have been his sister's head, but the result was blood everywhere. Shannon thought she was dying for sure.

Mother Sarah heard the screams and rushed to render assistance to Shannon, while brother Isaiah took off running as far from the scene as possible. He didn't fully understand what he had done, but knew he was in trouble. He had a habit of doing strange things, beginning with dragging his newborn sister off the bed, just as Mother Sarah entered the room to save her. That could have been a tragic experience in the family because Shannon may not have survived the fall from the bed.

Families, particularly families of color tend to make excuses for bad behavior from our male children. We even think some things boys do are funny. However, Shannon has clear thoughts since being rooted in Christ, and she feels certain, in retrospect, that elders rarely comprehended mental health issues when she was growing up. Young boys simply exhibited bad behavior, and everyone assumed he would grow out of it.

Sarah took all her children to school daily, and everyone stayed there except Isaiah. On one occasion, he entered the front door and exited the back door to walk two miles back home. He got a whipping, and didn't do that again. However, at age seven, Isaiah was bitten by a dog. He was riding his bike, and a dog running in the neighborhood chased him. It caught Isaiah and bit his legs, for no apparent reason. That turned into one of several hospital emergency room visits.

A more serious occurrence came the next year, when Isaiah was hit by a car. He was running after a cousin who was going to a local convenience store. When he got to the corner, Isaiah never stopped. He ran right into the street where a car was coming. It knocked him fifty feet into the air, and when his body landed on the pavement, he was still. His cousin quickly ran to get Mom Sarah, who performed mouth-to-mouth resuscitation in an effort to revive her son. Neighbors gathered quickly, and were praying out loud as the police and ambulance arrived.

The professionals were able to get a slight pulse, and they rushed Isaiah to the hospital. He stayed there about four months, after being in a coma for three weeks. There was chaos in the family, as everyone tried to survive day-to-day, while worrying that they might lose their young loved one.

Isaiah simply woke one day. He had to see a physical therapist in order to regain his ability to move and walk correctly. He also saw a neurological therapist, who told the family he didn't know if Isaiah would ever regain his intellectual abilities. Some of his verbal responses were delayed.

However, he did recover to the point where he seemed normal in his thinking and speaking. Shannon thinks God was attempting throughout Isaiah's young life to show the family that he had some special needs. It was, in fact, bizarre for a child to run into a busy street without even a slight hesitation. While the adults didn't grasp the possibility that God was speaking to them through their son's behavior patterns, they did surround Isaiah with more attention than they gave his siblings.

Isaiah went back to school, and finished fourth grade. He went on to finish elementary and middle school, played basketball and earned fairly good grades in his academics. The first three years of high school were uneventful, but in his senior year, he found the "wrong crowd." He started smoking, drinking and using drugs.

At the point where Isaiah needed crack cocaine, he only had to turn to some older family members to supply his drugs. At that time, there was so much family dysfunction that the drug problem seemed under control. Isaiah joined his older sister, Shirley in stealing household items to sell for drugs. He never graduated from high school.

A combination of pressures, both external and internal caused Isaiah to exhibit dangerous behavior towards his immediate family. He became physically abusive, emotionally aggressive, and uncontrollable. Even Mom Sarah was unable to reach him to turn him from the destructive path he was on. The only alternative was to have Isaiah committed to a mental institution. He was about twenty years old at the time.

Shannon believes that Isaiah was possessed with the kind of demons spoken about throughout the *Holy Bible*. Unclean spirits cause havoc in persons' lives, and Isaiah became the victim of this. Nevertheless, in the medical world, there needed to be a diagnosis "approved" by the professionals in that field. So Isaiah was labeled "Schizophrenic." He was treated medically for this disease.

Just as many members of Shannon's family have turned to Jesus Christ to be their Savior and daily companion in times of troubles, Shannon firmly believes that intercessory prayer may help Isaiah more than the drugs he has received over a period of years in the confined facility where he lives. That was not an option then, but it is now.

God has shown this extended family His grace and mercy through miracles, signs and wonders. Different family members have found Christ at the point where each was ready to receive Him. Collective and consistent prayer will bring Isaiah where God would have him to be.

Both Shannon and Shirley agreed to lead their brother, Isaiah through the "Sinner's Prayer." In Romans 10:9-10, we read, *"That if thou shalt confess with thy mouth the Lord Jesus and shalt believe in thine heart that God has raised him from the dead, thou shalt be saved. For with the heart man believeth unto righteousness and with the mouth confession is made unto salvation."*

The sisters had often discussed their separate prayers for Isaiah, and finally Shirley suggested they bring the "Sinner's Prayer" before Isaiah. God had lain upon her heart to minister to her brother, in hopes he would understand the importance of being saved.

Shirley asked him directly, *"Isaiah, if you passed today or tomorrow, do you know if you will go to Heaven?"* He said, *"No."* She then asked if he believes in God, to which he responded, *"Yes."* Shirley spoke about the fact that Jesus died for our sins, He loves Isaiah, and He rose again so that Isaiah and all of us could have salvation. Isaiah agreed to everything Shirley had said.

He repeated everything Shirley uttered, showing that he understood the need for him to recognize the concept of Heaven, redemption, and salvation. Since he formally accepted the "Sinner's Prayer," Isaiah is more calm than before. He is able to leave the institution to visit the family. God is at work in the lives of all the members of Shannon's family. This is the reason she placed Isaiah's story last in her book. He may be the catalyst for God to reach every single member of this special, brave family.

EPILOGUE

My family has taken the bold step of gathering everyone available over four generations, to sit together and talk about the generational curses of sexual abuse, verbal abuse, under-education and miscommunication that have plagued us until now. Collectively, our honesty about the most painful details of each of our lives has been the key to stopping all of these generational curses.

Like all families, we have had dysfunction, trouble, unbearable sorrow and gladness, too. But through it all, we used to believe that everything happening to us was fate, and we were helpless to impact our fate. Stresses were pushed aside for pretended normalcy. Sexual abuse, common in most families, was a subject never to be addressed.

Yet those hurting found no outlet to express what they felt internally after being physically violated. No healing could take place. I realize now that only God holds all the pieces of the puzzle, which I discovered through fervent prayer.

But God....I have come to believe, after writing this book, that each member of my family had to endure whatever God chose for us to endure, so that today, we could be made whole. We are operating in God's purpose because we made the sincere effort to understand one another, to understand ourselves, and most importantly, to forgive every member of my family for every offense, known and unknown. *"And we know that all things work together for the good to them that love God, to them who are the called according to His purpose."* (Romans 8:28)

Because we were determined to work through our pain to get to a place of joy, my large family has broken the generational curses intended to run through our family until the end of time. This was not easy, and my perseverance was a key ingredient in bringing us to the realization that we had an urgent message to convey to readers. It is my hope that readers of BREAKING *GENERATIONAL CURSES* will take the brave step to emulate what my family has done. The rewards are immeasurable!

"I have fought a good fight. I have finished my course. I have kept the faith. Henceforth, there is laid up for me a crown of righteousness which the Lord, the righteous judge shall give me at that day, and not to me only, but to all them also that love His appearing." (2 Timothy 4:7-8)

THE END

REFERENCES

The *Holy Bible:* New King James Version. (2016).

Jimmy Ruffin - What Becomes Of The Broken Hearted - YouTube
https://www.youtube.com/watch?v=2vf3ZE7CLg0

HOW YOU CAN REACH THE AUTHOR

If I can support others who are coping with breaking generational curses within your families, I invite you to reach out to me via my contact information below. I'm available for motivational speaking engagements, book signings, book club gatherings, Open Mike/Spoken Word readings, or intimate conversations with individuals or groups of persons experiencing the manifestations of generational curses.

Blessings,
Minister Shannon D. Brown

Mbrown465@cfl.rr.com
Call: 407-538-7702

P. O. Box 707
Apopka, Florida 32703

Made in the USA
Middletown, DE
14 October 2016